THE
COMMUNITY
COLLEGE
STORY

George B. Vaughan

The American Association of Community Colleges (AACC) is the primary advocacy organization for the nation's community colleges. The association represents more than 1,100 two-year, associate degree–granting institutions and more than 11 million students. AACC promotes community colleges through six strategic action areas: national and international recognition and advocacy, learning and accountability, leadership development, economic and workforce development, connectedness across AACC membership, and international and intercultural education. Information about AACC and community colleges may be found at www.aacc.nche.edu.

Design: Brian Gallagher Design
Editor: Deanna D'Errico
Printer: Graphic Communications, Inc.

Community College Press
American Association of Community Colleges
One Dupont Circle, NW
Suite 410
Washington, DC 20036

Printed in the United States of America

ISBN 0-87117-372-7

Contents

Tables and Figures

Foreword

In the more than a decade since *The Community College Story* was first published, higher education in general and community colleges in particular have faced an array of new challenges. Broad demographic shifts across the nation, urgent and changing workforce needs, and the need to respond to both business and societal needs in what is now a global economy and a world culture are key among them. During this decade of dramatic change, community colleges have not only met these challenges effectively but they have also continued to progress in the midst of growing enrollments and declining resources. What sustains the continued success of community colleges even while the landscape has shifted is that the fundamental mission has not changed: Community colleges continue to offer open, affordable access to higher education, regardless of the vagaries of the economy; provide comprehensive services that benefit not just the individual student but also whole communities; and, foremost, maintain an unswerving commitment to teaching and learning.

In the first six chapters of this new edition, readers will again find a concise overview of what community colleges are and what they do, along with updated demographic, enrollment, and financial statistics. In the all-new concluding chapter, "Facing the Challenges Ahead," readers will also find an analysis and forecast of the most salient issues that the colleges must face now and into the future. As it has been for more than four decades, AACC is proactively engaged in anticipating and addressing issues and conditions to advance the work of the colleges.

AACC is indebted to George B. Vaughan for undertaking the revision of this seminal monograph. His understanding of how community colleges have evolved, combined with a lifelong commitment to their mission, contribute to the clear and contextual portrait *The Community College Story* provides.

George R. Boggs
President and CEO
American Association of Community Colleges

The Community College

1

In addition to offering credit and noncredit courses to a broad constituency, many community colleges serve as cultural, social, and intellectual hubs in their communities. For the purposes of this discussion, a community college is defined as a regionally accredited institution of higher education that offers the associate degree as its highest degree; however, today, in a number of states community colleges offer the bachelor's degree as well.

Most community colleges are public and receive financial support from public tax dollars. Community colleges primarily serve commuter students, and most community colleges do not have residential facilities. Every community college has its own culture and serves a unique geographic area and clientele. Today, however, at many community colleges this clientele includes people training to work in the global economy.

Regardless of their geographic region and clientele, community colleges share many of the same values, goals, and ideals for themselves and their students. Community colleges are distinguished from other institutions of higher education by their commitment to open access, comprehensiveness in course and program offerings, and community building. These commitments shape the role and scope of community colleges.

Table 1.1
Number of Community Colleges: 1901–2005

Year	# of Colleges
1901	1
1910	25
1920	74
1930	180
1940	238
1950	330
1960	412
1970	909
1980	1,058
1990	1,108
2000	1,155
2004	1,158
2005	1,186

Source: AACC (2006)

Table 1.2
Undergraduate Fall Enrollment: 1993–2002

Year	Community Colleges	4-Year Colleges
1993	5,580,860	6,950,883
1994	5,561,476	6,899,283
1995	5,475,961	6,926,327
1996	5,508,223	6,929,410
1997	5,537,978	6,931,884
1998	5,533,383	7,113,957
1999	5,573,398	7,186,072
2000	5,942,371	7,356,758
2001	6,231,837	7,634,556
2002	6,562,386	7,853,688
Change 1993–1998	-0.9%	2.3%
Change 1998–2002	18.6%	10.4%
Change 1993–2002	17.6%	13.0%

Source: NCES (2004b)

The Mission

2

B roadly stated, the community college mission is to provide access to postsecondary educational programs and services that lead to stronger, more vital communities. The way in which individual community colleges achieve this mission may differ: Some colleges emphasize college transfer programs; others emphasize technical education. The commitment to offering courses, programs, training, and other services, however, is essentially the same for all community colleges. The mission of most community colleges is shaped by these commitments:

*   Serving all segments of society through an open-access admissions policy that offers equal and fair treatment to all students.
*   Providing a comprehensive educational program.
*   Serving the community as a community-based institution of higher education.
*   Teaching and learning.
*   Fostering lifelong learning.

Open Access and Equity

Access has been a major theme in American higher education since the end of World War II, and community colleges have been at the center of the nation's commitment to providing universal higher education. Community colleges have not always been open-access institutions, however. Three events contributed to making them so.

First, the children born to returning veterans of World War II—baby boomers—reached college age during the 1960s. Along with their parents, many of whom attended college with the help of the GI Bill, the baby boomers came to realize that their future opportunities would be closely linked to a college education. Second, the civil rights movement and advocacy for the rights of women and minorities broke down some of the barriers for disadvantaged groups.

Eliminating poverty and ignorance became important national goals of the Great Society envisioned by President Lyndon B. Johnson and other national leaders who promoted education, including higher education, as the most important means of achieving these goals. Third, the demands for political and social action during the 1960s and early 1970s resulted in a federal commitment to increase financial aid for higher education. The Higher Education Act of 1965, the 1972 amendments, and subsequent legislation at the national level made it possible for virtually anyone who could establish the need to receive financial assistance to attend college. The Higher Education Act, along with other federal and state programs, continues to provide financial assistance to students.

Open access to higher education, as practiced by the community college, is a manifestation of the belief that a democracy can thrive, indeed survive, only if people are educated to their fullest potential. Basic to the community college mission, then, are open-access admissions policies and fair and equal treatment of all students. Maintaining a low tuition rate and offering program choices achieve access; equity is achieved by removing barriers to access for those segments of society traditionally underserved by higher education.

Access and equity mean more than just open admissions. They mean having a college within commuting distance of most residents and giving students choices in what they study. Open access and equity mean that once a student is enrolled, the college provides support services, including counseling, academic advising, and financial aid, helping to ensure that every student has the opportunity to succeed academically. Many colleges offer child care, flexible scheduling, and distance education as part of their efforts to serve a population with diverse needs. Open access and equity mean that men and women from all ethnic, social, and economic backgrounds can afford to attend the community college and that no one is discriminated against in any academic program or service offered by the college.

Community colleges' commitment to open access in their admissions policies is perhaps the most misunderstood concept associated with these colleges. Open access does not mean that anyone can enter any program without the competencies required for effective learning. The prerequisites for entering the college transfer program at a community college are no different than they are at most four-year colleges and universities. The same is true of students entering any number of professional programs, such as nursing. Nevertheless, the community college differs from many institutions in the nation and in the world in the following way: Rather than turn away people who do not have the prerequisites for college-level work, the community college offers avenues for students to obtain the necessary prerequisites.

The Key

One way to illustrate the community college's commitment to access is to imagine each student having a key that represents educational achievement. A student who approaches a community college will find the main door open and therefore will not need the key to enter. A student who ultimately wishes to earn a bachelor's degree, however, will look for the door labeled College Transfer, which does require a key in the form of prerequisites such as college preparatory mathematics. If the student's key will not open the College Transfer door, there are alternatives, such as short-term training leading to immediate employment, for which the student's key may be compatible. Or the student can find the door labeled Developmental and Pre-College Courses. Like the door to the college, this one is open and does not require a key. Consequently, after completing developmental courses, the student may find it possible to open the door to College Transfer and continue on the path to a degree.

Access does not mean that anyone can enter any program without the necessary prerequisites but that options are available. Furthermore, community colleges must offer comprehensive programs with alternatives in order to fulfill the promises of access and equity. ✎

Comprehensiveness

The second commitment on which the community college mission rests, and one that relates to both open access and equity, is the commitment to ensure comprehensiveness in the college's program offerings. In addition to fulfilling the traditional university-parallel function of offering the first two years of the bachelor's program, community colleges offer much more. Indeed, in order to meet the needs of communities and to offer students the programs they want, some community colleges are offering four-year degrees in fields such as teacher education and business.

Although it is impossible and unnecessary for all community colleges to offer all programs, students must have choices in what they study for a community college to accomplish its mission. Without choice in program and course offerings, open access and equity lose much of their meaning. For example, if the college transfer program is the only program offered, the college is not an open-access institution because students have no choice in programs. Many students who come to the community college do not meet the academic requirements for the transfer program; thus, if that program is their only choice, the door to the college is closed to them, and open access is little more than a hollow promise.

To understand why comprehensiveness is so important to the community college, one has only to consider student goals and community needs. By broadening program offerings, community colleges have extended educational opportunities to millions of students ignored by other higher educational institutions. Some students want and need programs that lead quickly to employment. Others have the desire and the opportunity to pursue careers that require lengthier periods of schooling.

Community Based

It is no accident that the word *community* is part of the community college's name. *Community based* means that a college is committed to serving the needs of a designated geographic area, often called the college's service area or service region. Although the definition of what it means for a community college to serve its community has changed over the years—including an expansion of the definition of service area as a result of online learning—to be effective, the community college will see its mission as primarily one of providing education to its local community, including educating people to survive and thrive in a global economy.

Although needs are as diverse as the communities served by community colleges and may change over time, most communities have many needs in common and expect their college to meet those needs. Most communities want programs that permit students to transfer into a bachelor's degree program. Most want vocational and technical training, often including training that meets the specific needs of local and international businesses and industries. They expect a choice of credit and noncredit courses that lead to certificates, degrees, and diplomas. Most want the college to offer developmental courses that will help students qualify for college-level work.

Most communities want courses and activities that meet the recreational, social, and cultural needs of the community. Although cultural and social activities may not be part of a college's formal educational program, such activities enhance education and community life. Most observers agree that it is important for community colleges to sponsor art exhibits, sports events, concerts, drama productions, health fairs, community forums, and other activities that enrich the lives of the people served by the college. The decision to sponsor one event rather than another may be the result of a broad need in the community (a health fair, for example) or may be the result of an individual or group's desire to sponsor an activity. Whatever the reason, it is important that a college respond to the community's professed needs, thereby enhancing the college's mission.

Programs and activities overlap, and sometimes there is a fine line between an activity that is part of a formal education program or simply a community service. Colleges seek to remain flexible enough to respond to diverse community needs while maintaining integrity as institutions of higher education.

Teaching and Learning

The community college is devoted first and foremost to teaching and learning. Although publishing in academic periodicals is not mandatory for faculty, most community college leaders encourage faculty members to do so: Outstanding teachers must be devoted scholars, keeping up with their fields and sharing new developments with colleagues and students. The most important challenge for community college instructors is to develop the ability to adjust styles of teaching to the diverse learning styles of students.

Fostering Lifelong Learning

In the past, people may have assumed that education was an activity a person engaged in for a certain number of years, and, when that person graduated, he or she would never return to the classroom. Now, however, more people see learning as a lifelong pursuit. Many find they must continue to engage in formal learning activities, such as those offered at the community college, to keep up with the skills and knowledge required for their jobs or in order to be responsible and productive citizens.

The community college's commitment to lifelong learning encompasses an almost limitless number of credit and noncredit courses, activities, and programs designed to enhance the lives of the people in the college's service region for as long as they have the desire to learn. Students, many of whom are older adults, return to the classroom to learn new job skills and improve existing ones. A recent trend is the growing number of students returning to community college after completing a master's or other advanced degree.

One of the strengths of the community college is that it makes little distinction between the lifelong learner and the full-time student in terms of the programs and courses in which students may enroll. Many of the courses and programs lifelong learners choose are the same as those designed for degree-seeking students. As older adults return to the community college to upgrade their skills or learn new ones, the distinction between the adult learner and the full-time younger student diminishes.

Implementing the Mission

3

The community college achieves its mission through a number of programs, activities, and services. These include college transfer programs, occupational-technical programs, developmental education, community services including employee training, and a variety of support services.

College Transfer Programs

The great majority of the nation's community colleges offer transfer programs through which students can complete the first two years of college. Students enrolled in transfer programs take courses almost identical to those they would take in a bachelor's degree program at a four-year college or university. Most of the courses are in the humanities, mathematics, sciences, and social sciences.

Community college transfer programs enjoy great success. Some states accept transfer students earning the associate degree into the four-year university system without question. Most students who take the first two years of the four-year degree at a community college are successful in transferring their work to both private and public four-year institutions. U.S. Department of Education studies indicate that the academic records of community college students who transfer tend to compare favorably with those of the students who began their academic careers at four-year institutions.

Occupational–Technical Programs

Occupational–technical education programs have been an important part of the public community college's curriculum since the 1920s, and they remain essential for the United States to compete in a global economy and for American workers to keep up with the changing skills needed in the workplace. In the beginning, most public junior colleges limited their occupational programs to teacher training, office skills, and the agricultural sciences. Over time, many of these programs evolved into baccalaureate programs and have been replaced at community colleges by programs in fields as diverse as early childhood education, office management, laser optics, medical and computer technologies, auto body repair, and fire science.

A series of federal programs—including the Vocational Act of 1963, its 1968 and 1972 amendments, and the Carl D. Perkins Act of 1984 and its later reauthorizations—have strengthened community colleges' capacity to develop new occupational–vocational programs. Vocational education has been elevated to the four-year level in those community colleges that now offer the bachelor's degree in fields such as teacher education, business, and some technologies.

Why Do Community Colleges Offer Developmental Education?

For one reason or another, millions of people in the United States reach adulthood without the education necessary to compete for high-skilled jobs. Workers laid off from jobs midway through their career may lack the skills to reenter the ever-changing workforce. Immigrants who lack English-language skills also may struggle to find employment. The number of unskilled jobs is decreasing and the number of high-skilled jobs increasing. If people continue to reach adulthood without the education needed for 21st-century jobs, unemployment among unskilled workers will rise, contributing to poverty and social unrest. For the nation to remain strong, the population must be educated to meet the needs of 21st-century employers.

Community colleges have the tools to help respond to many of the nation's education needs. All community colleges offer remedial education—developmental education—that is designed to bring students up to a level of competency necessary to participate in college-level courses or to gain productive employment. Whatever the reason that students have not met the academic requirements previously, community colleges offer developmental education that prepares them for college-level work.

An educated population is vital to the nation's economic, political, and social health. As institutions devoted to universal higher education, community colleges offer developmental education as an important part of fulfilling the community college mission. ✑

Developmental Education

A number of terms are used to describe pre-college courses offered at community colleges—for example, *developmental education*, *remedial education*, or *compensatory education*. Regardless of the name, courses that prepare students to enter college-level courses are an important part of a community college's offerings.

It is not possible to describe the students who require developmental courses in simple terms. Some of the brightest students enrolling in a community college may need precollege courses before enrolling in a degree program. For example, someone who has been out of the job market and without formal schooling for 10 years and who wishes to enroll in a community college nursing program may need precollege courses in mathematics or science. Students who may not have acquired basic skills because of language barriers, a learning disability, or other learning impediments brought on by various life circumstances may need courses in English, writing, or math. In general, it is the community college perspective that society cannot afford to leave anyone behind and that developmental education is a crucial part of the commitment to access, student success, and community building.

Table 3.1

Ten Most Frequently Awarded Community College Certificates and Degrees: 2002

Field of Study	Certificates	Associate Degrees	Total
Liberal arts and sciences, general studies, and humanities	3,659	196,358	200,017
Health professions and related sciences	64,880	65,197	130,077
Business management and administrative services	37,109	71,515	108,624
Protective services	17,483	15,103	32,586
Engineering and related technologies	78	1,586	28,847
Computer and information sciences	9,873	17,590	27,463
Mechanics and repairers	18,128	7,952	26,080
Vocational home economics	11,534	7,962	19,496
Visual and performing arts	2,465	11,740	14,205
Marketing operations/marketing and distribution	8,720	4,983	13,703
Total Awarded	173,929	399,986	601,098

Source: NCES (2004a)
Note. Certificates are for programs less than 4 years in length.

Community Service and Service Learning

Community service, or continuing education, is the most flexible and broad area of community college offerings. It includes courses and activities that are often paid for by participants rather than by tax dollars. Offerings may range from hobby courses such as floral arranging or automobile maintenance to training in information technology or emergency medical treatment. Business and industry look to community colleges to provide on-demand skills training for workers in their service area and for the global market. The colleges have the flexibility to respond quickly to the training needs of business and industry, in part because much of what is taught under the community services umbrella does not require approval by the governing board or state coordinating agency. Many community colleges enjoy highly successful relationships with businesses and industries in their service region and, in some cases, around the world.

Service learning is a teaching and learning strategy combining community service with classroom instruction, focusing on critical, reflective thinking as well as personal and civic responsibility. Service learning programs involve students in activities that address local needs while developing their academic skills and commitment to their community. Since 1994 AACC has promoted the value of service learning to the nearly 1,200 associate degree–granting institutions. According to three AACC national surveys, more than half of all community col-

Table 3.2
Top 15 Hot Programs at Community Colleges: 2004

Programs	Average Starting Salary
Registered nursing	$38,416
Law enforcement	$31,865
Licensed practical nursing	$27,507
Radiology	$35,612
Computer technologies	$35,469
Automotive	$32,498
Nursing assistant	$16,754
Dental hygiene	$35,956
Health information technology	$26,578
Construction	$34,414
Education	$30,810
Business	$31,366
Networking	$35,938
Electronics	$32,734
Medical assistant	$22,953

Source: McPhee (2004)

Note. Hot programs are those in which students, according to reporting colleges, are in high demand upon graduation. Data pertain to both for-credit and noncredit programs.

leges offer service learning in their curricular programs. Another 35% to 40% of colleges are interested in starting service learning initiatives.

Service learning is integrated across the disciplinary spectrum, from social sciences, languages, and humanities to allied health, math, science, and technology. College students serve at K–12 schools, social service and cultural organizations, senior centers, and environmental and health agencies. Training, technical assistance, and referrals are available, at little or no cost, from AACC and the Community College National Center for Community Engagement.

Support Services

The community college's open-access admissions policy has ethical implications as well as educational ones. The college has an ethical obligation to see that students who enroll have a reasonable chance of achieving academic success, assuming they do their part. To succeed academically, students often require a number of support services beyond classroom instruction. With this in mind, community colleges maintain learning resource centers containing books, films, videos, computers, online courses, and any number of materials and equipment that enhance learning.

In addition, community colleges provide a network of support services designed to provide students with assistance as they work toward their academic goals. Online course work may be available through writing laboratories, academic advising, personal and career counseling, employment advice, transfer

Table 3.3
Mean Earnings of Workers Aged 25 or Older, by Highest Level of Education Attained: 2002

Highest Level of Education Attained	Earnings
Less than 9th grade	$18,935
9–12 grade, no diploma	$22,463
High school diploma	$29,185
Some college, no degree	$35,370
Associate degree	$35,590
Bachelor's degree	$53,103
Master's degree	$60,726
Professional degree	$113,242
Doctorate	$89,638
Total	$39,849

Source: U.S. Census Bureau (2004)
Note. High school diploma includes GED or equivalency.

information for those wishing to pursue a bachelor's degree, career planning, financial aid counseling, and any number of services that help fulfill the promise of the community college's open door. Open-access admissions can succeed only if students receive the assistance they need for academic success.

Students and Faculty

4

For an idea of who attends community college, go to any town or city that has a community college, stand on a street corner, and watch people go by. Take away most people under 18 and most over 60, and the parade that passes will look much like students at a typical community college. Included will be men and women who work full time and part time, people from all walks of life and of diverse racial and ethnic backgrounds, unemployed and underemployed individuals, and recent high school graduates.

The ranks of students may include a medical technician wanting to keep up with the latest in the field, a factory worker seeking to upgrade skills, a retired person or homemaker needing to learn or upgrade computer knowledge in order to reenter the workforce, or traditional college students enrolled in the transfer program. The list is as long as the needs, desires, and dreams of people in towns across the nation. The common theme is that the students have discovered the community college and are using it to fulfill their educational needs.

To understand the perspective of today's community college students, as well as a growing number of four-year students, it is helpful to view them from a different perspective than the one through which college students are traditionally viewed. Traditional-age college students, those aged 17 to 21, are customarily perceived as being in a holding pattern, waiting until graduation to assume the rights and responsibilities that accompany full citizenship. Their role is one of student as citizen, with the student role dominant. One result is that the student-citizen is somewhat isolated from the real world of work (even though many such students have part-time jobs),

Figure 4.1
Community College Fall Enrollment by Age: 2001

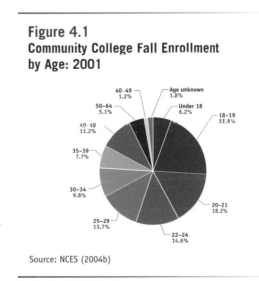

Source: NCES (2004b)

from family responsibilities, and from other rights and responsibilities that will come when that student finishes college.

Many community college students, especially the more than four million who attend college part time, have reversed the role of student-citizen to that of citizen-student. The citizenship role, rather than the student role, is dominant. The citizen-student is concerned with paying taxes, working full time, supporting a family, paying a mortgage, and other responsibilities associated with the everyday role of a full-time citizen. College attendance is important but often depends on the availability of money and time.

The citizen-student role has implications for how courses are taught (more emphasis on the students' experiences and knowledge), when they are taught (in the evening and on weekends, online anytime, with approximately 80% of the nation's community colleges offering online instruction), and, in some cases, by whom they are taught. As many community colleges have discovered, the citizen-student role requires an entirely different approach to providing extracurricular activities for most students. The single parent with small children who attends class one night a week is unlikely to

Figure 4.2
Community College Enrollment by Race/Ethnicity: 1993

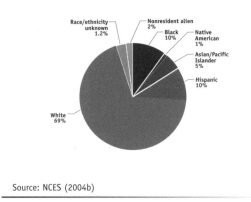

Source: NCES (2004b)

Figure 4.3
Community College Enrollment by Race/Ethnicity: 2002

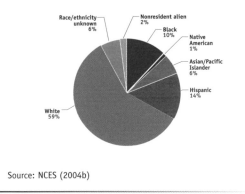

Source: NCES (2004b)

attend the Friday night dance at the college. The reporter on the local newspaper is unlikely to serve on the staff of the college newspaper.

It is not that the dance or the newspaper or any other activities are unimportant. It is that educating the citizen-student requires a different approach to enhance the college experience. While recognizing the needs of the citizen-student, the community college cannot neglect those students who attend the community college expecting a more traditional college experience, including extracurricular activities that afford opportunities to develop leadership and social skills. Meeting the needs of those students for whom the college experience is dominant requires planning, including academic advising and mentoring by faculty, just as is true for the student whose citizenship role is dominant. Because these students are often preparing to transfer to a four-year institution, they may require more attention than the student who is taking one course or noncredit courses.

Faces of the Future

Annually since 1999, AACC and ACT have been partnering on the groundbreaking study, Faces of the Future, which provides a complete profile of the student body—credit and noncredit—enrolled in community colleges. The study provides colleges, legislators, and the public with reliable and focused data describing the diverse clientele who find, in their local community college, the opportunity for growth and enhanced life options.

Community college students have a wide variety of demographic characteristics, goals, needs, and life circumstances. One group of students who are especially likely to be in community colleges are students whose parents have no postsecondary education experiences—first-generation students. According to the National Center for Education Statistics (2005), in 2003 first-generation students made up 45% of the public community college population (*Faces of the Future: A Portrait of First-Generation Community College Students* is available on AACC's Web site—see Nomi, 2005).

Faculty Dedicated to Teaching and Learning

Faculty, whether full-time or part-time, are the heart of a learning institution. Community colleges employ more than 114,000 full-time faculty and approximately 206,000 part-time faculty (NCES, 2004c). Most full-time faculty at community colleges have a master's degree, and an increasing proportion (17%) hold a doctoral degree (NCES, 2004c). Many community colleges have academic ranks (professor, associate professor, assistant professor, instructor) similar to faculty ranks at four-year institutions. Some community colleges have academic systems based on longevity, performance, and other factors that determine status and pay. Many community colleges grant academic tenure. Community colleges without a faculty tenure system have some means of reappointing faculty, such as a system of multi-year appointments or a ranking system that ensures job continuity, much like the civil service system. Some community college faculty members, both full and part time, belong to labor unions.

In keeping with the mission, community college faculty members' primary responsibility is teaching. In addition, faculty members hold regular office hours to work with students and advise them on their programs of study. Faculty members also work with students as sponsors of clubs, community service projects, newspapers, literary publications, and other extracurricular activities.

Many community college faculty members maintain ties to their disciplines through reading and writing and by attending the meetings of their professional associations. In addition to national organizations, most states have organizations devoted to the advancement of teaching in the community college. Many faculty members arrange for internships in businesses to ensure that what they teach is up-to-date and pertinent to current employment.

A large percentage (63%) of community college faculties are part time (NCES, 2003). Part-time faculty members teach for a number of reasons. Teaching is a way to fulfill a civic duty, is a forum for sharing knowledge with others, and is a way of facilitating learning. Most part-time faculty teach one to three courses per term (3–9 credit hours), whereas full-time faculty members usually teach five courses (15 credit hours).

By bringing specialties to the college that may not be available among full-time faculty, part-time faculty play an important role in assisting the community college to be a comprehensive institution of higher education. For example, most colleges would not have a full-time faculty member available to teach courses in real estate, whereas qualified instructors are readily available in any community with a viable real estate market. Similarly, a local banker can bring practical experience to the community college classroom that might be unavailable among full-time faculty. Many community colleges can offer certain specialized courses and programs only through the use of part-time faculty. For example, it is often necessary for a small college to employ part-time faculty members for courses in art, music, some languages, and technology fields.

As faculty members who joined community colleges during the boom years of the 1960s and 1970s began to retire, community colleges have been recruiting new instructors who are expected to have a command of technology to teach their courses effectively, many of which are now offered online. Faculty members today must understand and be committed to diversity in students, in their own ranks, in the community, and in the workplace. As the community college has evolved to play an important role in a world beyond its local community, faculty members too must evolve to understand, appreciate, and enhance that world.

Figure 4.4
Employment Status of Public Community College Students by Attendance Status: 2003–2004

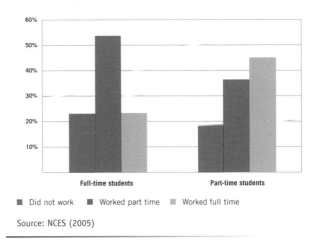

Source: NCES (2005)

An Opportunity to Excel

Many people begin their higher education at a community college and continue on to achieve national recognition in a variety of fields. Community colleges are proud of these outstanding alumni, who reinforce the fact that success is often a matter of personal commitment and taking advantage of the opportunities at hand.

One community college alumnus who made particularly valuable contributions was Jackie Robinson, who attended what was then Pasadena Junior College in California before going on to study at the University of California and then to make history as the first African American to play major league baseball. Robinson not only broke down the color barriers in baseball but frequently spoke out to help further the cause of civil rights. Household names such as Robinson and Calvin Klein are names of community college alumni. Countless more former students have excelled in their chosen fields, even if their achievements are less universally known.

K. Kristene Koontz Gugliuzza, MD, began her studies at Lake Land College in Illinois and went on to become one of only a small number of women kidney/pancreas transplant surgeons in the country. M. Anthony Burns, alumnus of Dixie College, Utah, became president and CEO of Ryder

Systems and showed community support and leadership in responding to the devastation of Hurricane Andrew by donating needed resources that Ryder could offer.

Flying seems to be an area to which outstanding alumni gravitate. Mildred "Micky" Axton, alumna of Coffeyville Community College in Kansas, was the first woman to fly a B-29 bomber. Astronaut Robert "Hoot" Gibson attended Suffolk County Community College in New York, and Fred Haise, who flew the famed Apollo 13 mission, attended Mississippi Gulf Coast Junior College. Eileen Collins, alumna of Corning Community College in New York, also became a NASA astronaut and in 1999 was named the first female U.S. Space Shuttle Commander.

Community college alumni have proved themselves worthy role models and valuable contributors to society. Meanwhile, each day community college students work toward their goals, whether or not they are widely celebrated. Rising the next step in a career path or learning the skills needed to win employment to support a family can be a personal if not public triumph. There are many paths to success, and those paths frequently and sometimes surprisingly start with a first step through a community college door. ✎

Funding and Governance

5

Community colleges receive most of their funding from federal, state, and local taxes, with by far the greatest support coming from state and local tax sources. On average nationally, community colleges receive approximately 42% of their funds from state taxes, 24% from local government, 18% from tuition and fees, 6% from the federal government, and 10% from other sources (Knapp, Kelly-Reid, & Whitmore, 2006). As is true with so much else about community colleges, funding is characterized by its diversity and varies from state to state and, in some cases, from college to college within a state. Whereas some community colleges receive large portions of their budgets from local sources, others receive little or no local tax support.

Tuition and fees, to a varying degree, provide an important source of income for all community colleges. On average nationally, public community colleges charge about $2,191 for tuition and fees annually (College Board, 2005). Nevertheless, tuition and fees charged at community colleges vary greatly. Among the states at the high end of the tuition scale are Massachusetts, Minnesota, New Hampshire, and New York. Among those at the lower end of the scale are California, North Carolina, and Texas.

Community colleges receive funds from other sources as well. For example, many community colleges offer noncredit courses and activities through their community services and continuing education divisions. Those taking courses or participating in the activity usually pay for these courses. Sometimes the courses are paid for by businesses that contract with the colleges to train or retrain workers for specific jobs. Contract training is a source of revenue for some community colleges.

Many community colleges are beginning to supplement their revenues by establishing educational foundations. Foundations are common for four-year colleges and universities but have been part of the community college picture only recently. These nonprofit organizations are incorporated to receive endowments and other types of funds for use by the community college with which they are affiliated. Some colleges place major emphasis on raising funds from private sources and are very successful in obtaining funds. Other colleges place little emphasis on private fundraising.

In the final analysis, the funding package depends on the social, political, and economic conditions as well as the funding history of a community college in a given state or even in a given geographic area within a state. Regardless of funding sources, community colleges have kept student costs relatively low. Community college presidents, the American Association of Community Colleges (AACC), and local and state political leaders seek to ensure that tuition and fees remain reasonable. Similarly, national political leaders have helped promote open access through student aid programs.

Community College Governance

In the academic world, governance is the process through which institutional decisions are made. Rules, regulations, laws, committees, formal and informal groups and leaders, organizational structure, and the history and culture of the institution influence the governing process. All of these components constitute the internal forces that affect a community college and its governance. Individuals and groups outside the institution also affect governance. The most important internal influence on governance is the formal organization, with the college president at its center. A critical external force, and one that has increased in importance in recent years, is state government. Especially important in influencing how community colleges are governed are state legislators and the governor's office.

Community colleges have formal organizational structures, just as companies and universities do. The president of the college, as chief executive officer, is responsible for the college's daily operation. In addition, community colleges have vice presidents, deans, department chairs, and others who organize and supervise administrative support for the faculty, staff, and students. Various committees, collegewide forums, college councils representing all segments of the college, and the president's cabinet enhance the governing process. Faculty members participate through service on committees and councils and by voicing their opinions at open forums. Many community colleges involve support staff in the governing process. On some campuses, both the support staff and the faculty belong to labor unions. These unions influence how the college is governed.

College presidents report to the board and are responsible for keeping the board informed and involved in those decisions that affect the direction and future of the college. In the case of some state systems, presidents report to a chancellor who, in turn, reports to the governing board. The president is responsible for seeing that the rules and regulations established by the governing board are followed. The president also has the responsibility for keeping the board informed about all aspects of the college's operation, often serving as secretary to the board. Some community college presidents are non-voting members of the governing board.

The effective president and board work together as a team, each recognizing and respecting the other's sphere of authority and responsibility. The governing board is legally responsible for the community college's well-being. The board makes the policies that the president implements and oversees. Governing boards approve budgets, programs, personnel appointments, campus development, long-range plans, and other actions that materially affect the operation of the college.

Effective boards usually do not become involved in the daily operation of the college, recognizing that this area is the president's responsibility. Community college governing boards are responsible for the employment, evaluation, and termination of the college president. In choosing the president, the board plays a major role in determining how the college is administered and led.

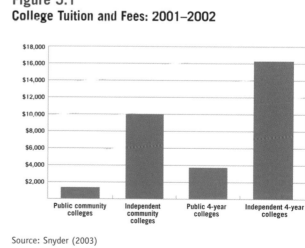

Figure 5.1
College Tuition and Fees: 2001–2002

Source: Snyder (2003)

Elected Boards

Some states have locally elected boards made up of individuals who reside in the college's service area. In many of these states, would-be trustees campaign for board membership, much as they would if they were running for any political office. They are elected for a given term and must seek reelection if they wish to continue to serve on the board. One argument for elected boards is that because the people elect them, they are responsive to and responsible to the people who elect them. The counterargument is that because voter turnout for board elections is usually small, those who do vote have an agenda in mind. Therefore, the elected board member may be under the influence of special interests. In any event, elected boards have built strong community college systems, including those in Kansas, Arizona, California, Michigan, and Texas.

Appointed Boards

Some states have locally appointed boards made up of people who reside in the college's service area. These boards may be appointed by the governor (the most common practice), by other political leaders, or by a combination of the two. Some educators believe that appointed board members will be loyal to the appointing official, not to the community college. But because appointed board members do not spend time and money on an election, they may have more time for college board work. States with appointed boards include Florida, Illinois, North Carolina, and Washington.

State Boards

State-level boards govern some states. State board members are usually appointed by the governor and serve for specific terms. In contrast to locally appointed and elected boards, state board members are selected from across the state. As a group, they do not reside in any single college's service area. Critics of state-level boards maintain that they erode local control of the college and that without local control the college will not serve its community as well as it would if its board members were from the college's service area. Some states with state-level boards have local college boards that represent local interests and advise the state board on local matters. As with locally appointed boards, some fear that the loyalty of state board members will be to the governor and not to the local colleges. States with state-level boards include Alabama, Virginia, and the State University of New York system.

A History of Innovation

6

Among the many innovations of the early 20th century were experiments in higher education, and many people and institutions contributed to a growth spurt in higher education in those years. One of the earliest public junior colleges grew out of the high school in Joliet, Illinois. In 1901, the Joliet Township school board authorized the offering of post-graduate education beyond high school course work. In 1916, the postgraduate division was separated from the high school and, in 1917, was formally renamed Joliet Junior College. As the nation's oldest continuously operating public two-year college, Joliet was important for several reasons:

- It demonstrated that a well-equipped public high school could offer college-level courses equal to those offered by a university.
- It demonstrated the feasibility and desirability of using tax dollars to offer postsecondary education in the community.
- The needs of the community helped shape the courses and programs offered by this community-based institution.
- The acceptance of courses offered at Joliet by the University of Chicago and Northwestern University illustrated the feasibility and practicability of transferring courses from a public junior college to a university.

In 1907, California passed legislation authorizing high schools to offer the first two years of college; in 1917, the state legislature reaffirmed the right of local school districts to organize public junior colleges. In 1921, the legislature authorized the establishment of independent junior college districts governed by local boards. With the passage of enabling legislation in California in 1907 and in Kansas and Michigan in 1917 and with the growth of public junior colleges, the movement gathered steam. During the first quarter of the 20th century, Texas, Oklahoma, Illinois, Mississippi, Missouri, Iowa, Kansas, and Michigan were among the states that established public junior colleges. Today, every state has one or more public community colleges.

A National Association

Early in the 20th century, junior colleges felt a need to join together to articulate the role and mission of the two-year college. A group of presidents representing public and independent junior colleges met in St. Louis in 1920 at a meeting called by the U.S. Commissioner of Education. As a result of this meeting, an organization was conceived that would function as a forum for the nation's two-year colleges. The group agreed to meet again the next year in Chicago. The result was the founding of what became known as the American Association of Junior Colleges (AAJC). In 1930, the first issue of *The Junior College Journal* was published. In 1972, the name of the national organization was changed to the American Association of Community and Junior Colleges (AACJC), reflecting the community orientation of most public two-year institutions. In 1992, the name was changed to its current form, the American Association of Community Colleges.

Today, AACC has more than 1,100 member colleges. The association provides a forum for discussing community college issues and serves as the point of contact for the nation's federal and state agencies, the office of the president of the United States, state governors, international governments, scholars of higher education, the news media, businesses, and others who wish to learn more about community colleges. AACC is the chief advocate and lobbyist for community colleges at the national level.

GI Bill

As World War II was winding down, the nation's policymakers struggled to determine what to do with the millions of servicemen and servicewomen who would soon return to civilian life. Recalling the prewar economic depression, the nation's leaders and citizens feared there would not be enough jobs to absorb those returning from military service. The nation's political leaders had an answer that would delay the returning military personnel's entry into the job market, improve their skills, and reward them for serving their country: Send them to college. Congress passed the Servicemen's Readjustment Act in 1944, a major milestone in federal financing of education. Known as the GI Bill of Rights, this act helped break financial and social barriers for millions of Americans who had served in World War II. The public junior college, along with the rest of higher education, received boosts in enrollment as a result of the federally funded bill.

The bill provided what amounted to a scholarship for every eligible veteran and set a precedent for the student financial aid that exists today, especially in the idea that students should not be barred from college attendance for financial reasons and that they should have choices in the colleges they attend and the programs they study. The philosophy of the GI Bill and of later student aid programs has had, and continues to have, enormous impact on community college enrollment, in the diversity of students enrolled, and on programs and mission.

Truman Commission Report

Early in 1947, less than two years after the end of World War II, the President's Commission on Higher Education for American Democracy issued what is commonly called the Truman Commission Report, written to help ensure that higher education would play a major role in preserving and enhancing the democratic ideals for which the nation's citizens had fought during the war. The commission asserted that 49% of high school graduates could profit from two years of education beyond high school and sought a way to offer more opportunities for college attendance.

The commission, chaired by junior college advocate and then president of the American Council on Education, George Zook, believed that an important way to break down the barriers to higher education was to establish a network of publicly supported two-year institutions. The commission used the term *community college* to describe these institutions. Community colleges, the commission suggested, should place major emphasis on working with the public schools. They should be within reach of most citizens, charge little or no tuition, serve as cultural centers for the community, offer continuing education for adults as well as technical and general education, be locally controlled, and be a part of their state's and the nation's higher education system.

Growth in the 1960s and 1970s

After a period of slow growth in the 1950s, during which community colleges struggled to find secure footing and a number of independent junior colleges closed or converted to four-year institutions, the 1960s ushered in an extraordinary era of new growth for the nation's public two-year colleges). Between 1960 and 1970, 457 new public community colleges opened throughout the country.

Factors that helped fuel the boom of colleges in the 1960s included legislative actions such as the passage of the Higher Education Act, which provided greater federal support to education. California's Proposition 13, passed in 1978, signaled a trend toward states rather than local entities paying an increasing share of community college costs. It also resulted in a shift toward more state control and less local control of community colleges. Social forces that helped encourage growth in the colleges include a peak in the number of baby boomers coming of age and the end of school segregation in the South, which bolstered commitment to access and equity.

Increased Size and Scope

During the second half of the 20th century, community colleges grew more comprehensive in their offerings. They remained committed to providing the first two years of a liberal arts baccalaureate education, but they also responded to economic downturns with commitment to workforce retraining and community development. Local and state governments and the federal government offered varying levels of support, and some colleges thrived more than others.

In 1988, the report *Building Communities: A Vision for a New Century* resulted from a series of meetings sponsored by the W. K. Kellogg Foundation and the Metropolitan Life Foundation and facilitated by the American Association of Community and Junior Colleges Commission on the Future of Community Colleges. The report listed recommended goals for community colleges and introduced the idea that "the word *community* should be defined not only as a region to be served, but also as a climate to be created."

Sponsors and Partners

A number of corporations and educational affiliates have shown long-term support for community colleges. The W. K. Kellogg Foundation and the Ford Foundation, for example, have contributed considerable resources to efforts furthering higher education for all citizens. Grants from corporations such as Microsoft and government entities such as the Department of Labor and the National Science Foundation help fund vital programs in workforce, advanced technology, and teacher training. The American Council on Education and ACT, Inc., are two of the many education organizations with whom AACC works. Collaboration is the goal and the essential ingredient for bringing about positive changes for colleges, communities, and students.

Facing the Challenges Ahead

7

Thomas P. "Tip" O'Neill, Jr., the late speaker of the U.S. House of Representatives, liked to say, "All politics is local." For community colleges, all education is local. As heads of institutions designed to attend to local residents' higher education needs, community college leaders decipher trends— whether international, national, or state—according to the implications for their communities and campuses. Today when issues regularly cut across disciplines and geographic boundaries, viewing matters through the lens of local concerns does not mean community colleges are provincial. AACC provides services that facilitate community colleges' responses to both the routine and extraordinary circumstances of college management. AACC also advocates nationally for the resources that community colleges need to carry out their many missions. This dynamic interplay between community-based educational activities and national advocacy will intensify in the coming years as several of the major issues that surfaced since 2000 continue to challenge community colleges collectively and individually.

Access to higher education through community colleges has gained wide acceptance in principle. The reality of access via community colleges' open admissions policies will continue to be tested, however, by constraints on public funding, rising tuition, increases in enrollments, changes in technologies, and the need to serve legions of underprepared students. In recent years, it has become apparent that it is not enough for community colleges to welcome all potential learners. Community colleges must also have mechanisms in place to help students persist and reach their educational goals. Through its active partnership with Lumina Foundation for Education, other funders such as the KnowledgeWorks Foundation and Nellie Mae Education Foundation, and other national partners working together on the Achieving the Dream Initiative, AACC is part of an ambitious research-based project to increase student success. AACC will continue to seek increased funds for federal programs like Pell Grants, which help people attend their local community colleges.

Demographic changes are expected to generate shifts in student populations and campus leadership in coming years. With baby boomers' children reaching adulthood, enrollments are increasing at all types of higher education institutions. But, with higher education costs climbing, more of these traditional, college-aged students are seeing the wisdom of starting their postsecondary studies at community colleges. Community colleges' historically high enrollments of minority students are expected to grow as the nation's minority population, particularly its Hispanic population, grows. The return of more adults to community colleges for new high-tech competencies also fuels enrollment growth, and the colleges are expanding their engagement of learners 50 and older who, far from being ready for traditional retirement, are seeking new options for their third stage of living and learning. The influx of students is expected to coincide with the retirement of many senior administrators and faculty members. In the coming years, AACC will continue to encourage the expansion of professional development programs to nurture a new generation of highly qualified, diverse community college leaders.

Achieving the Dream: Community Colleges Count

Achieving the Dream is a major, national partnership initiative geared toward increasing student success at community colleges, particularly underserved, ethnically diverse, and nontraditional students. The initiative's work comprises five major strands: promote and sustain institutional change, develop policy, engage the public, build knowledge, and enhance partners' capacity. In its first two years, Achieving the Dream awarded grants to 35 colleges in seven states. Colleges are charged with developing a culture of evidence based on data in order to improve the persistence and success of students in remedial and gatekeeper courses, as well as certificate and degree programs. AACC's role includes hosting Strategy Institutes for participating colleges, promoting Achieving the Dream's goals nationally, and developing a sophisticated interactive Web site for showcasing student success stories and tracking institutional progress and relevant state policies. Lumina Foundation for Education initiated the program and funded its first phase. The Nellie Mae Education Foundation and the KnowledgeWorks Foundation have joined the effort, which is managed by MDC, Inc. In addition to AACC, other national partners include the Community College Leadership Program of the University of Texas at Austin, the Community College Research Center of Teachers College at Columbia University, Jobs for the Future, MDRC, and Public Agenda. ✑

Global economic competition and political events are increasing the need for an international component in the education of all community college students. Being a citizen now involves understanding the complexity of world affairs and the interdependence of the world's peoples. New technologies that make it cheaper and easier to communicate all over the world have generated fierce competition and new ways of working that place even small, rural businesses in the international marketplace. These changes will continue to affect those who employ community college graduates and reverberate in curriculum changes across the country. The U.S. government has also called on community colleges and other higher education sectors to welcome more international students as a way of promoting peace and understanding. As is pointed out in a joint statement by AACC and the Association of Community College Trustees (2006), "Enhancing global awareness is not only in the community's self-interest, but it also serves the nation as a whole. The ability to understand, appreciate, and communicate effectively—irrespective of national and cultural origins—frees the forces of economic development and allows ideas, capital, and innovation to move unimpeded…Community colleges are, in effect, 'stewards to the world.'" To assist colleges as they pursue these broader ideas of community, AACC will continue its efforts to attract more international students to community college campuses, support outreach to international educators, and encourage international faculty and student exchanges.

Financial pressures at local, state, and national levels of government are pushing community colleges toward entrepreneurial endeavors and collaborative partnerships. In the coming years, community colleges will engage more actively in fundraising and establish or strengthen foundations to encourage support from individuals, corporations, and other entities. Community colleges are also expected to expand their searches for grants and other funding sources. Although the competition for funding may increase, there are promising signs that higher education in the future will be a more collaborative enterprise. Talk about K–16 educational considerations is slowly moving beyond rhetoric to activities that combine the strengths of various education sectors and their community partners. If this trend continues, long-sought seamless articulation and other benefits may follow.

AACC plans to continue to use partnerships to maximize its advocacy for community colleges. By cultivating connections with other national and international educational organizations, AACC advances community colleges' positions on issues of mutual interest and draws attention to the importance of community colleges in higher education. For instance, AACC and the six largest higher education associations in the United States are working together to advocate for common objectives in the reauthorization of the Higher Education Act.

The Leading Forward Initiative

A critical factor in the community college's future is leadership. Retirements are leading to high levels of turnovers among leaders at all levels. Who will the next leaders be? Will they be committed to the community college's historic mission of ensuring access? How will they be prepared to meet current and future challenges? With generous support from the W. K. Kellogg Foundation, AACC is addressing these questions through its Leading Forward initiative. After a board task force began looking at the challenges in earnest in 2000, AACC has documented the turnovers in presidential leadership and seen steady increases in the numbers of women and minority leaders, and in the numbers of new first-time CEOs. To understand how leaders are being prepared, the initiative compiled a database of leadership programs offered by AACC Affiliated Councils, private-sector organizations, universities, and others. The initiative also analyzed current next-generation university-based community college leadership programs, similar programs supported by Kellogg in the 1960s and 1970s, and the burgeoning "grow your own" leadership programs launched more recently by individual colleges and states. A series of Leading Forward leadership summits in 2003 led to the development of field-supported Competencies for Community College Leaders. By 2005, the competencies—grouped under organizational strategy, resource management, communication, collaboration, and community college advocacy—were being used to help structure credit and non-credit leadership development programs across the country. ✎

Natural disasters and terrorism have challenged community colleges and people in unexpected and unprecedented ways since 2000. Although no one can predict the future, community colleges' adroit responses to recent tragedies will inform and guide other community colleges during difficult times in the future. The Borough of Manhattan Community College's willingness to be a staging area for workers after the terrorist attack at the World Trade Center in 2001 was an instinctive and generous contribution to its injured city. Similarly, the leadership provided by the Louisiana Community and Technical College System and the Mississippi State Board for Community and Junior Colleges after hurricanes devastated the Gulf Coast in 2005 exemplified community colleges' rapid and community-minded responses to crises.

Disaster preparation on campuses will continue to be a priority for community college leaders in the coming years. Nationally, community colleges will have a key role in homeland security through expanded educational programs for police officers, firefighters, airport security personnel, cybersecurity technicians, and others. As it has in the past, AACC will advocate for the needs of community colleges and their students, whatever the challenge. Following the hurricanes, AACC lobbied for fully portable federal financial aid for students. It also sought private and public funds to help displaced students continue their education and help devastated campuses to rebuild and expand construction technician and other training that residents needed to restore their lives. AACC has also made sure that the homeland security appropriations bill recognizes community colleges as the preferred provider of first-responder training.

Preserving access, improving student success rates, responding appropriately to changing demographics, increasing global competition, and addressing pressing financial concerns are the obvious issues on the horizon for community colleges. Even when unforeseen events occur, students and communities can be assured that their educational needs will be the priority of community colleges. The successful evolution of community colleges depends on the development of a new generation of leaders.

Milestones in Community College History

1862 *Passage of the Morrill Act*
With its emphasis on agriculture and the mechanical arts, the Morrill Act of 1862, often referred to as the Land Grant Act, expanded access to public higher education, introduced the teaching of new types of courses, and included types of students previously excluded from higher education.

1874 *The Kalamazoo Decision*
The Michigan Supreme Court ruled that local school districts could construct and operate comprehensive high schools from public school funds. This precedent-setting decision opened the way to the development of the modern, comprehensive high school, which would, by the opening of the 20th century, provide many public community colleges with their initial home.

1901 *Founding of Joliet Junior College*
One of the earliest beneficiaries of the construction of large, modern high schools was Joliet Junior College. Founded under the influence of William Rainey Harper, president of the University of Chicago, Joliet Junior College is the oldest continuously existing public two-year college in the nation. While the junior college's courses were initially mixed in with those of the Joliet high school, by 1915 the junior college's enrollment had grown to such an extent that it necessitated the addition of a "junior college wing." This was the nation's first major facility constructed specifically for use by a public junior college.

1904 *The Wisconsin Idea*
The University of Wisconsin emphasized that its mission was to assist the general public through extension services and to provide support to the state government. The university declared that the entire state was its campus. Today, most community colleges view individual service regions as their campuses.

1917 *Adoption of Junior College Accreditation Standards*
The North Central Association of Colleges and Schools
established specific standards for the accreditation of public and private junior colleges. These standards, governing
such areas as admissions policies, faculty qualifications,
and minimum funding levels, not only brought a degree of
uniformity to the young junior college movement but
demonstrated the willingness of and capacity for junior
colleges to participate in America's unique system of institutional self-regulation.

1918 *Founding of Phi Theta Kappa (PTK) Honor Society*
PTK was founded to recognize and encourage academic
achievement by two-year college students and provide
them with opportunities for individual growth and development in academics, leadership, and service.

1920– *Founding of the American Association of Junior Colleges*
1921 Called together by Philander Claxton, U.S. commissioner
of education, and his higher education specialist, George
Zook, more than 25 public and private junior college leaders met in St. Louis in 1920 to discuss the role of the junior college in American higher education. The group met
again in Chicago in 1921. The result was the founding of
the American Association of Junior Colleges (AAJC).
Designed to assist the presidents of the rapidly growing
number of junior colleges in advocating for the colleges,
AAJC became a forum for community college issues and
a source of mutual support for its members at a time when
the potential of the junior college was not widely under-
stood or appreciated.

1921 *California Legislation Fostering Independent Community
College Districts*
Using proceeds from the federal Oil and Mineral Act, the
California legislature created a Junior College Fund, the
nation's first, to support the operation of locally governed

junior college districts operating independently of the public high schools. California's Junior College Act of 1921 came to serve as a model for other states as they sought to put junior colleges on a sound fiscal and policy footing.

1928 *The First State Junior College Board*
Mississippi was the first state in the nation to organize a statewide governing board with specific oversight responsibility for the public junior colleges within its boundaries. The state's governing board worked closely with elected local boards to develop a strong network of public junior colleges that effectively balanced transfer and vocational programs.

1930 *The Asheville Decision*
Even as late as 1930, many state legislatures had yet to adopt specific legislation permitting communities to organize public junior colleges. This legal oversight did not deter communities, which organized junior colleges without explicit legal authority, much as they had organized high schools in the preceding century. The right of a community to take such a step was challenged in Asheville, North Carolina, with the state supreme court eventually ruling in favor of the community and its right to meet the education needs of its citizens as it best saw fit. This decision did much to secure the legal standing of those public junior colleges that were still being operated without the benefit of state legislation.

1930 *Launch of the* **Community College Journal**
The first issue of the *Community College Journal* was published by Stanford University Press, under the joint auspices of AACC (then AAJC) and the School of Education at Stanford.

1944 *Passage of GI Bill of Rights*

The U.S. Congress passed the Servicemen's Readjustment Act, popularly known as the GI Bill, to provide financial assistance for veterans of World War II who wished to pursue higher education. Building on smaller federal student aid programs developed at the end of the Great Depression, the GI Bill represented the federal government's first attempt to provide student aid on a large scale, helping to break down the economic and social barriers to attending college.

1947 *Higher Education for American Democracy*

Published by the President's Commission on Higher Education for American Democracy, the Truman Commission Report, as it is commonly known, called for several things, including the establishment of a network of public community colleges that would charge little or no tuition; serve as cultural centers; be comprehensive in their program offerings with an emphasis on civic responsibilities; and serve the area in which they were located. The commission helped popularize the term *community college*.

1958 *Introduction of Associate Degree Nursing Programs*

With funding support from the W. K. Kellogg Foundation and Rockefeller family, community colleges in New York, California, Florida, and other states introduced two-year programs leading to an associate degree in nursing that entitled degree holders to sit for licensure as professional nurses.

1960 *W. K. Kellogg Foundation Support of Community College Leadership Development*

The W. K. Kellogg Foundation announced a series of grants to be used to establish university centers preparing a new generation of two-year college leaders. In all, 12 universities established junior college leadership programs. Hundreds of future deans and presidents would eventually graduate from the Kellogg Junior College Leadership Programs.

1960 *California Master Plan for Higher Education*
The three segments of California public higher education—community colleges, comprehensive colleges and
universities, and the University of California—agreed to a
voluntary plan to divide responsibility for the state's rapidly growing number of undergraduates and provide the
state's residents with the broadest possible range of educational opportunity without wasteful competition among
the sectors.

1963– *Federal Aid to Higher Education*
1965 With the adoption of the Higher Education Facilities Act
of 1963 and the first Higher Education Act of 1965, the
federal government dramatically expanded its direct aid to
community colleges and their students. Through the
Facilities Act of 1963, communities were given the means
to construct new campuses and enlarge existing facilities.
Through the Higher Education Act of 1965 and its subsequent reauthorizations, the federal government provided a
range of direct grants and loans to students based on need
as a means of lessening the barrier of cost to higher education access.

1968 *Creation of the League for Innovation in the Community
College*
B. Lamar Johnson founded the League for Innovation to
promote experimentation and innovation in community
colleges. The League limits its membership to 20 colleges,
which are self-selected and expected to demonstrate out
standing commitment to cutting-edge thinking in leadership and direction of community colleges. Results and
information are shared with community colleges across
the nation and internationally through a League Alliance
made up of more than 800 institutions from 16 different
countries.

1970 *Open Admissions at City University of New York*
Breaking with a long-established tradition of selective admissions, the City University of New York ended its policy of granting admission to only the most academically gifted graduates of New York's public high schools and guaranteed admission to all high school graduates. This policy change led to a rapid increase in enrollment, the introduction of large-scale developmental programs, and the organization of innovative community colleges in communities with the greatest economic need.

1971– *Federal Aid for Strengthening Tribal Colleges*
1978 Beginning with Navajo Community College in 1971, AACC assisted in winning federal aid for the construction and maintenance of community colleges operating under the jurisdiction of Native American tribes. These efforts culminated in 1978, with the adoption of the Tribally Controlled Community College Assistance Act and the expansion of the community college to previously under-served communities throughout the West.

1972 *Name Change for the Association*
The American Association of Junior Colleges changed its name to the American Association of Community and Junior Colleges to reflect the broadening terminology used by the institutions.

1972 *Creation of Affiliated Councils*
Councils are organizations whose purposes are consistent with AACC's and whose programs contribute to and significantly benefit the association and its members. Beginning in 1972, councils that meet certain criteria may be eligible for affiliate council membership, which brings with it an added measure of recognition and benefits.

1972 *Establishment of Association of Community College Trustees (ACCT)*
ACCT is the national organization for the nation's community college lay trustees. More than 6,500 trustees govern the nation's community colleges. ACCT places major emphasis on providing trustees with the knowledge, skills, and avenues for influencing public policy at national and state levels. ACCT works closely with AACC in shaping, achieving, and promoting the community college mission.

1972 *Establishment of the Basic Educational Opportunity Grant (Pell Grant)*
Through the reauthorization of the Higher Education Act, the Basic Educational Opportunity Grant, which later became the Pell Grant, was created. Two million community college students now receive these need-based grants.

1975 *Creation of the Presidents Academy*
Composed of chief executives of AACC member colleges, the Presidents Academy provides opportunities for career development through workshops and meetings. Workshops vary in focus but are designed to enhance leadership skills, technology awareness, and public policy awareness in top college officials.

1978 *Proposition 13 in California*
The passage of Proposition 13 in California signaled the beginning of an increased demand by the public for greater accountability from its public institutions. Community colleges have been in the forefront in adopting strategies for ensuring the most effective use of public funds in an era of fiscal constraint.

1978 *Establishment of National Institute for Staff & Organizational Development (NISOD)*
NISOD is dedicated to the professional development of community college faculty, administrators, and staff and to the continued improvement of teaching and learning. With more than 700 members around the world, NISOD is the outreach vehicle and service arm to the Community College Leadership Program at The University of Texas at Austin, a doctoral-level training program for presidents, vice presidents, and deans.

1985 *Establishment of Community College Press*
Under this imprint, AACC publishes books, reports, and monographs on topics of interest to community college professionals.

1988 *Commission on the Future of Community Colleges Report*
The commission's report, *Building Communities: A Vision for a New Century*, defined *community* "not only as a region to be served, but also as a climate to be created." Community colleges were challenged to assume a leadership role in creating a renewed climate of community in their service regions.

1988 *Launch of the* **Community College Times**
The *Community College Times* (then called the *Community, Technical, and Junior College Times*) was first published in December 1988 as a 20-page "special showcase edition." The first official biweekly issue came out the following month, January 1989.

1992 *Second Name Change for the Association*
The association changed its name to the American Association of Community Colleges in an effort to unify its diverse membership of technical, junior, and community colleges.

1992 *Scientific and Advanced Technology Act*
This landmark legislation authorized the program that has since become known as the Advanced Technological Education program. The program has spawned a highly productive relationship between the National Science Foundation and community colleges across the nation.

1996 *AACC Web Site Launched*
In 1996, AACC launched its Web site. Redesigned in 2004, the site currently comprises more than 16,000 individual pages and gets 7,200 unique visitors a day.

1998 *Hope Scholarship and Lifetime Learning Tax Credits Established*
The Hope "scholarship" is a tax credit available to eligible students during their first two years of postsecondary education. The tax credit is available for two tax years to those students who have not completed the first two years of postsecondary education. The lifetime learning credit is available for education beyond the first two years of college.

1998 *Workforce Investment Act*
This law substantially alters the federal government's role in job training, adult education, and vocational rehabilitation. Community colleges will still have a major role in the delivery of training services, but most of the funding will follow the participants. Training will be delivered primarily through Individual Training Accounts (or vouchers) and one-stop career center systems.

1998 *Carl D. Perkins Vocational and Technical Education Act Reauthorization*
The Perkins Act represents the major federal commitment to vocational education activities. The reauthorization removes set-asides historically included in the law for special populations and provides states flexibility in determining how best to spend Perkins dollars, while requiring that

specific accountability measures be met. Community colleges are considered important providers of postsecondary vocational education.

2000 *New Expeditions Report*
The W. K. Kellogg–funded New Expeditions project aimed to set a vision and strategic direction for the nation's community colleges for the first part of the 21st century. Relying on input from the field and critical analysis of trends, the project culminated in *The Knowledge Net: Connecting Communities, Learners, and Colleges,* which challenged community colleges through a series of recommendations for action.

2001 *Community College Centennial*
As the community college turned 100, it continued to evolve, responding to the needs of society at large while retaining its core commitment to equal access. In a century of growth, community colleges became the largest sector of higher education, serving close to half of all U.S. undergraduates.

2004 *Creation of the Community-Based Job Training Grant Program*
This Department of Labor initiative is directed exclusively at community colleges and is designed to enhance the ability of community colleges to deliver high-quality job training programs in high-demand fields.

2006 *Establishment of the Congressional Community College Caucus*
This 80-member bipartisan caucus is designed to highlight the contributions, needs, and goals of community colleges, as well as the role that they play in our nation's economy and social life. By holding briefings and circulating materials of interest, the caucus raises the profile of community colleges in the capital and help members of Congress and their staff better serve community colleges.

References

American Association of Community Colleges. (2006). AACC membership database [Data file]. Washington, DC: American Association of Community Colleges.

American Association of Community Colleges and Association of Community College Trustees. (2006). *Building the global community: Joint statement on the role of community colleges in international education.* [Brochure]. Available from www.aacc.nche.edu

College Board. (2005). *Trends in college pricing: 2005.* New York: Author. Available from www.collegeboard.com

Knapp, L. G., Kelly-Reid, J. E., & Whitmore, R. W. (2006). *Enrollment in postsecondary institutions, fall 2004; graduation rates, 1998 & 2001 Cohorts; and financial statistics, fiscal year 2004* (NCES 2006-155). Washington, DC: U.S. Department of Education, National Center for Education Statistics. Available from http://nces.ed.gov/pubsearch/pubsinfo.asp?pubid=2006155

McPhee, S. (2004). *Hot programs at community colleges.* Washington, DC: Community College Press.

National Center for Education Statistics. (2003). *Integrated postsecondary education data system (IPEDS) fall staff survey* [Data file]. Washington, DC: U.S. Department of Education.

National Center for Education Statistics. (2004a). *Integrated postsecondary education data system (IPEDS) completions survey* [Data file].Washington, DC: U.S. Department of Education.

National Center for Education Statistics. (2004b). *Integrated postsecondary education data system (IPEDS) fall enrollment survey* [Data file]. Washington, DC: U.S. Department of Education.

National Center for Education Statistics. (2004c). *National study of postsecondary faculty: 2004.* Washington, DC: U.S. Department of Education. Available from the Data Analysis System Web site, www.nces.ed.gov/das

National Center for Education Statistics. (2005). *National postsecondary student aid study: 2003–2004.* Washington, DC:

U.S. Department of Education. Available from the Data
Analysis System Web site, www.nces.ed.gov/das

Nomi, T. (2005). *Faces of the future: A portrait of first-generation
community college students.* Washington, DC: American
Association of Community Colleges. Available from
www.aacc.nche.edu

Snyder, T. D. (2003). *Digest of education statistics: 2002* (NCES
2003-060). Washington, DC: U.S. Department of
Education, National Center for Education Statistics.

U.S. Census Bureau. (2004). *Educational attainment in the United
States: March 2001 and March 2002.* Washington, DC:
U.S. Department of Commerce.

Resources

Publications

Adelman, C. (1992). *The way we are: The community college as American thermometer.* Washington, DC: U.S. Department of Education.

Adelman, C. (2006, February). *The toolbox revisited: Paths to degree completion from high school through college.* Washington, DC: U.S. Department of Education. Available from www.ed.gov/rschstat/research/pubs/toolboxrevisit/index.html

American Association of Community Colleges. (2001). *America's community colleges: A century of innovation.* Washington, DC: Community College Press.

American Association of Community Colleges. (2003). *State-by-state profile of community colleges* (6th ed.). Washington, DC: Community College Press.

American Association of Community Colleges. (2004). *Competencies for community college leaders.* Washington, DC: American Association of Community Colleges. Available from www.ccleadership.org/resource_center/competencies.htm

American Association of Community Colleges. (2006). *First responders: Community colleges on the front line of security).* Washington, DC: Community College Press. Available from www.aacc.nche.edu/firstresponders

American Association of Community Colleges & American Association of State Colleges and Unversities. (2004). *Improving access to the baccalaureate.* Washington, DC: Community College Press. Available from www.pathtocollege.org

Baker, G. A., III (Ed.). (1994). *A handbook on the community college in America.* Westport, CT: Greenwood Press.

Blocker, C. E., Plummer, R. H., & Richardson, R. C., Jr. (1965). *The two-year college: A social synthesis.* Englewood Cliffs, NJ: Prentice Hall.

Boggs, G. R. (2006). *Handbook on CEO–board relations and responsibilities.* Washington, DC: Community College Press.

Bogue, J. P. (1950). *The community college.* New York: Teachers College Press.

Brick, M. (1963). *The American Association of Junior Colleges.* New York: Teachers College Press.

Brint, S., & Karabel, J. (1989). *The diverted dream: Community colleges and the promises of educational opportunity in America, 1900-1985.* New York: Oxford University Press.

Cohen, A. M., & Brawer, F. B. (1987). *The collegiate function of community colleges.* San Francisco: Jossey-Bass.

Cohen, A. M., & Brawer, F. B. (2003). *The American community college* (4th ed.). San Francisco: Jossey-Bass.

Community College Survey of Student Engagement. (2002). *Engaging community colleges: A first look.* Austin, TX: Author.

Community College Survey of Student Engagement. (2003). *Engaging community colleges: National benchmarks of quality.* Austin, TX: Author.

Deegan, W. L. (1985). *Renewing the American community college.* San Francisco: Jossey-Bass.

Diener, T. (1986). *Growth of an American invention: A documentary history of the junior and community college movement.* Westport, CT: Greenwood Press.

Eells, W. C. (1930). *Bibliography on junior colleges.* Washington, DC: Government Printing Office.

Fields, R. (1962). *The community college movement.* New York: McGraw-Hill.

Frye, J. H. (1992). *The vision of the public junior college, 1900–1940.* Westport, CT: Greenwood Press.

Garms, W. I. (1977). *Financing community colleges.* New York: Teachers College Press.

Gillett-Karam, R., Roueche, S. D., & Roueche, J. E. (1991). *Underrepresentation and the question of diversity: Women and minorities in the community college.* Washington, DC: Community College Press.

Gleazer, E. J., Jr. (1980). *The community college: Values, vision, and vitality.* Washington, DC: American Association of Community Colleges.

Harlacher, E. L. (1969). *The community dimension of the community college.* Englewood Cliffs, NJ: Prentice Hall.

Hussar, W. J. (2005). *Projections of education statistics to 2014* (NCES 2005-074). Washington, DC: U.S. Department of Education, National Center for Education Statistics.

Johnson, B. L. (1952). *General education in action.* Washington, DC: American Council on Education.

Kalick, R. (1992). *Community college libraries: Centers for lifelong learning.* Metuchen, NJ: Scarecrow Press.

Knoell, D. M. (1966). *Toward educational opportunity for all.* Albany, NY: State University of New York.

Levin, J. S. (2001). *Globalizing the community college: Strategies for change in the twenty-first century.* New York: Palgrave.

McCabe, R. H. (2000). *No one to waste: A report to public decision-makers and community college leaders.* Washington, DC: Community College Press.

McCabe, R. H. (2003). *Yes we can! A community college guide for developing America's underprepared.* Phoenix, AZ: League for Innovation in the Community College and American Association of Community Colleges.

McCabe, R. H., & Day, P. R., Jr. (Eds.). (1998). *Developmental education: A twenty-first century social and economic imperative.* Phoenix, AZ: League for Innovation in the Community College.

McPhail, C. J. (Ed.). (2005). *Establishing and sustaining learning centered community colleges.* Washington, DC: Community College Press.

Medsker, L. L., & Tillery, D. (1971). *Breaking the access barrier: A profile of two-year colleges..* New York: McGraw-Hill.

Monroe, C. R. (1972). *Profile of the community college.* San Francisco: Jossey-Bass.

Palinchak, R. S. (1973). *The evolution of the community college.* Metuchen, NJ: Scarecrow Press.

Parnell, D. (1985). *The neglected majority.* Washington, DC: Community College Press.

Phillippe, K. A., & González Sullivan, L. (2005). *National profile of community colleges: Trends and statistics* (4th ed.).

Washington, DC: Community College Press.

Romano, R. M. (Ed.). (2002). *Internationalizing the community college.* Washington, DC: Community College Press.

Rosenfeld, S. (2006). *Cool community colleges: Creative approaches to economic development.* Washington, DC: Community College Press.

Roueche, J. E., Baker, G. A., III, & Rose, R. R. (1989). *Shared vision: Transformational leadership in American community colleges.* Washington, DC: Community College Press.

Roueche, J. E., & Jones, B. R. (Eds.). (1999). *The entrepreneurial community college.* Washington, DC: Community College Press.

Roueche, J. E., Milliron, M. D., & Roueche, S. D. (2003). *Practical magic: On the front lines of teaching excellence.* Washington, DC: Community College Press.

Roueche, J. E., & Roueche, S. D. (1999). *High stakes, high performance: Making remedial education work.* Washington, DC: Community College Press.

Thornton, J. W. (1960). *The community junior college.* New York: Wiley and Sons.

Vaughan, G. B. (1998). *The community college presidency at the millennium.* Washington, DC: Community College Press.

Vaughan, G. B., & Weisman, I. M. (1997). *In the nation's service: Community college trustees.* Washington, DC: Association of Community College Trustees.

Witt, A. A., Wattenbarger, J. L. Gollattscheck, J. E., & Suppiger, J. E. (1994). *America's community colleges: The first century.* Washington, DC: Community College Press.

Zoglin, M. L. (1976). *Power and politics in the community college.* Palm Springs, CA: ETC Publications.

Web Sites

ACT
www.act.org

American Association of Community Colleges
www.aacc.nche.edu

Association of Community College Trustees
www.acct.org

The College Board
www.collegeboard.com

Community College National Center for Community Engagement
www.mc.maricopa.edu/engagement

Community College Research Center
http://ccrc.tc.columbia.edu

Federal Student Aid
www.ed.gov/about/offices/list/fsa

League for Innovation in the Community College
www.lcague.org

National Center for Education Statistics
http://nces.ed.gov

National Institute for Staff & Organizational Development
www.nisod.org

Peterson's (education resources)
www.petersons.com

U.S. Bureau of Labor Statistics
www.bls.gov

U.S. Census Bureau
www.census.gov

U.S. Department of Education
www.ed.gov

About the Author

George B. Vaughan is president emeritus of Piedmont Virginia Community College and professor emeritus of higher education at North Carolina State University. He currently serves as editor of the *Community College Review*. His specialty is working with public community colleges in any number of capacities. Vaughan served as chief academic officer at two community colleges before becoming a community college president. He served as president of Piedmont Virginia Community College in Charlottesville, Virginia, for 11 years and as founding president of Mountain Empire Community College in Big Stone Gap, Virginia, for 6 years. A national study named him one of the 50 most effective community college presidents in the nation. During his tenures as president, he began his scholarly work on community college presidents and trustees, work that he continues today.

Vaughan has written more than 100 articles and a dozen books related primarily to community colleges. His books on the community college presidency won two national awards. He received the AACC's highest leadership award, as well as a number of other national awards. He served on the board of directors of AACC for three terms. He has worked with governing boards, faculty members, and administrators in a number of states on issues related to leadership, scholarship, and the history of the community college. He has taught a number of graduate courses related to higher education in the United States and has served as advisor to many graduate students.

Vaughan received a bachelor's degree in economics from Emory and Henry College, a master's degree in history from Radford University, did two years of doctoral work in history at the University of Tennessee, and received a PhD in higher education from Florida State University.